HAL•LEONARD®
BASS
PLAY-ALONG

AUDIO
ACCESS
INCLUDED

VOL. 5

FUNK

T0040778

To access audio visit:
www.halleonard.com/mylibrary

7692-7853-4208-8762

ISBN 978-0-634-09006-2

HAL•LEONARD®
CORPORATION
7777 W. BLUEMOUND RD. P.O. BOX 13819 MILWAUKEE, WI 53213

Visit Hal Leonard Online at
www.halleonard.com

contents

Bass Notation Legend

Bass music can be notated two different ways: on a *musical staff*, and in *tablature*

THE MUSICAL STAFF shows pitches and rhythms and is divided by bar lines into measures. Pitches are named after the first seven letters of the alphabet.

TABLATURE graphically represents the bass fingerboard. Each horizontal line represents a string, and each number represents a fret.

3rd string, open   2nd string, 2nd fret   1st & 2nd strings open, played together

HAMMER-ON: Strike the first (lower) note with one finger, then sound the higher note (on the same string) with another finger by fretting it without picking.

PULL-OFF: Place both fingers on the notes to be sounded. Strike the first note and without picking, pull the finger off to sound the second (lower) note.

LEGATO SLIDE: Strike the first note and then slide the same fret-hand finger up or down to the second note. The second note is not struck.

SHIFT SLIDE: Same as legato slide, except the second note is struck.

TRILL: Very rapidly alternate between the notes indicated by continuously hammering on and pulling off.

TREMOLO PICKING: The note is picked as rapidly and continuously as possible.

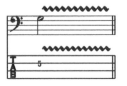

VIBRATO: The string is vibrated by rapidly bending and releasing the note with the fretting hand.

SHAKE: Using one finger, rapidly alternate between two notes on one string by sliding either a half-step above or below.

NATURAL HARMONIC: Strike the note while the fret hand lightly touches the string directly over the fret indicated.

Harm.

MUFFLED STRINGS: A percussive sound is produced by laying the fret hand across the string(s) without depressing them and striking them with the pick hand.

BEND: Strike the note and bend up the interval shown.

1/2

BEND AND RELEASE: Strike the note and bend up as indicated, then release back to the original note. Only the first note is struck.

1/2

RIGHT-HAND TAP: Hammer ("tap") the fret indicated with the "pick-hand" index or middle finger and pull off to the note fretted by the fret hand.

LEFT-HAND TAP: Hammer ("tap") the fret indicated with the "fret-hand" index or middle finger.

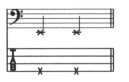

SLAP: Strike ("slap") string with right-hand thumb.

T

POP: Snap ("pop") string with right-hand index or middle finger.

P

Additional Musical Definitions

(accent)	• Accentuate note (play it louder)	
(accent)	• Accentuate note with great intensity	
(staccato)	• Play the note short	
D.S. al Coda	• Go back to the sign (𝄋), then play until the measure marked *"To Coda"*, then skip to the section labelled *"Coda."*	

Fill   • Label used to identify a brief pattern which is to be inserted into the arrangement.

• Repeat measures between signs.

1. **2.**   • When a repeated section has different endings, play the first ending only the first time and the second ending only the second time.

Brick House

Words and Music by Lionel Richie, Ronald LaPread, Walter Orange, Milan Williams, Thomas McClary and William King

*Key signature denotes A Dorian.

§ Chorus

brick house. _

See additional lyrics

She's might - y, might - y _____ just let - tin' it all _ hang out. _ Ah, she's a

brick house. _ I like

la - dies stacked _ and that's a fact. _ Ain't hold - in' noth - in' back. _ Ow, she's a

How can she lose ___ with the stuff she use? Thir-ty-six,

D.S. al Coda

twen-ty-four, ___ thir-ty-six. Ow, what a win-ning hand ___ ful. She's a

Coda

Verse
Am7

built like an Am-a-zon. ___ 2. Mm, _____ the clothes she wear, ___ her

sex-y ways ___ make an old man ___ wish for

9

young-er days, __ yeah, __ yeah.   She __ knows she's built   and

knows how   to   please. ___   Sure 'nough can knock a   strong __

Chorus
Am

man to his knees. _'Cause she's a   brick   house. __   Yeah, __

___ she's might-y, might-y ___   just   let-tin' it all __ hang out. __   Hey,

10

Bridge

built like an Am - a - zon.___ Yeah.

Shake it down, shake it down, shake it now,   now.___

___ Shake it down, shake it down,   shake it now,   now.___

Shake it down, shake it down, shake it now,   now.___

Shake it down, shake it down,   shake it, shake it.

___ Shake it down,   shake it down.   Shake it.

Interlude

Oh,   a

Outro

brick   house. ___

Repeat and fade

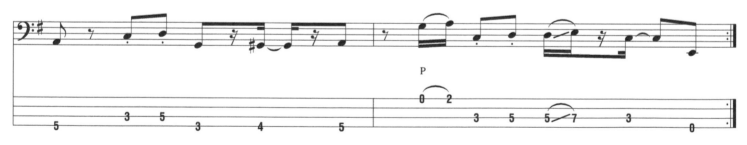

Additional Lyrics

Chorus   She's a brick house.
           She's mighty, mighty just lettin' it all hang out.
           Ah, she's a brick house.
           Oh, I like ladies stacked and that's a fact.
           Ain't holdin' nothin' back.
           Oh, she's a brick house.
           Yeah, she's the one, the only one
           Built like an Amazon.

Get Off

Words and Music by Carl Driggs and Ismael Angel Ledesma

Verse

1. Cra - zy la - dies are at our dis - cre - tion so we can get off.
2. *See additional lyrics*

We keep un - der the sheets with two love - lys

2nd time, substitute Fill 1

so we can get off. Sly looks that we get from

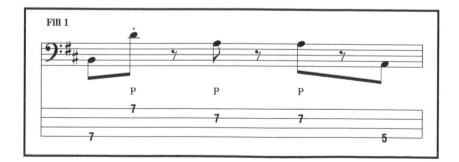

Fill 1

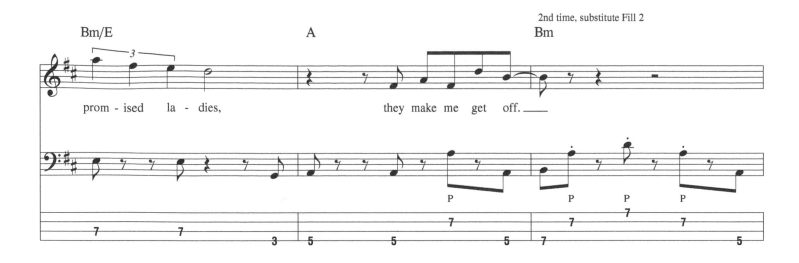

prom - ised la - dies, they make me get off.____

Take it from girls ____ with our i-mag - i - na - tion so we can get off.__

Pre-Chorus

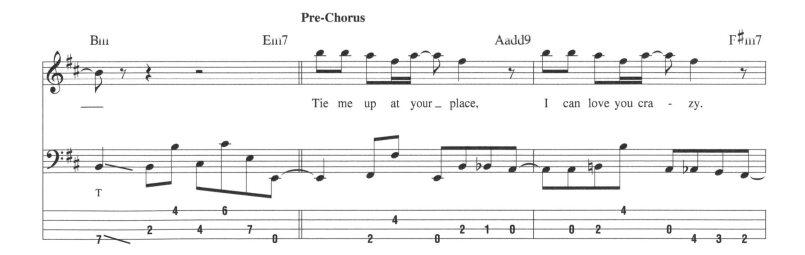

___ Tie me up at your __ place, I can love you cra - zy.

Fill 2

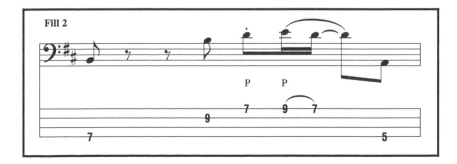

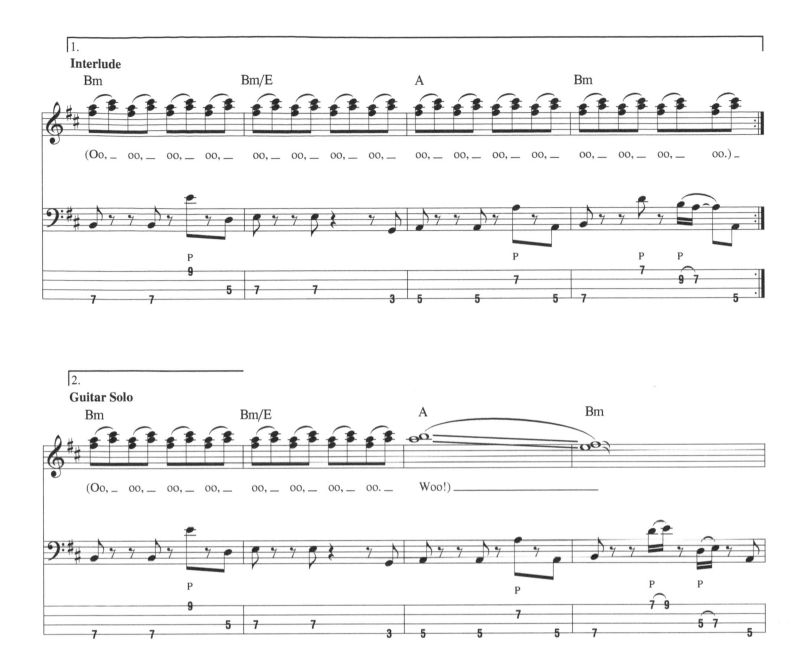

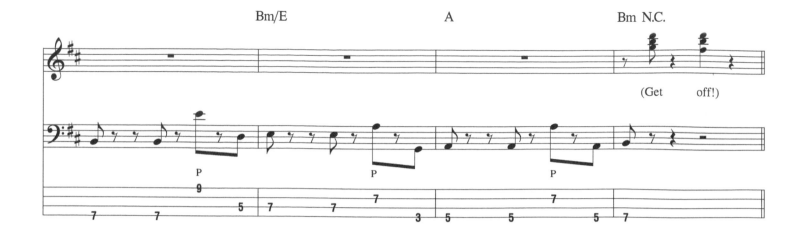

(Get off!)

Interlude

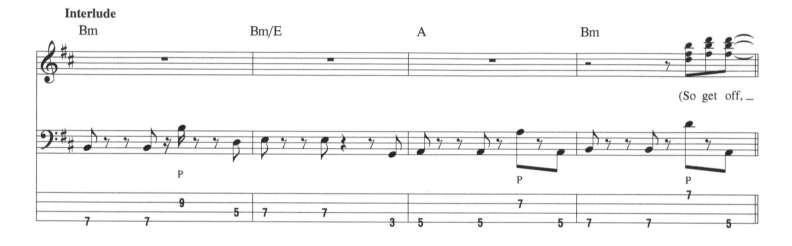

(So get off, __

Outro-Chorus

__ go get off, __ to get off, _____ to get,

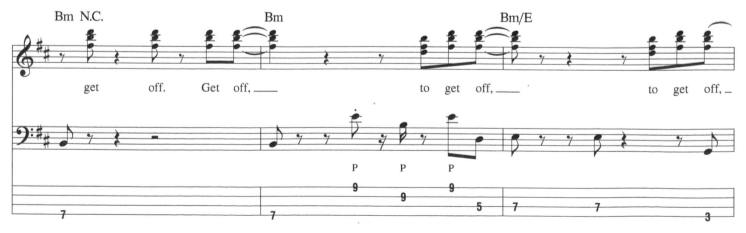

get off. Get off, __ to get off, __ to get off, __

20

to get off. ___ To get off, ___ to get off, ___

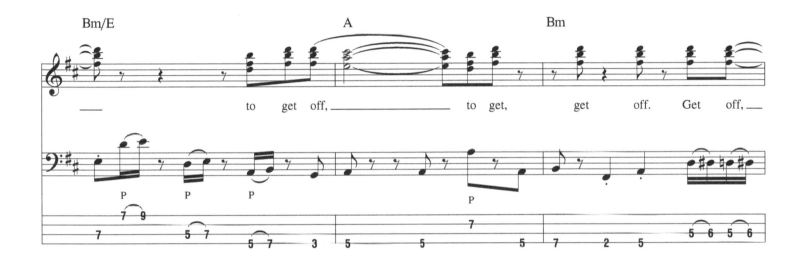

___ to get off, ___ to get, get off. Get off, ___

Fade out

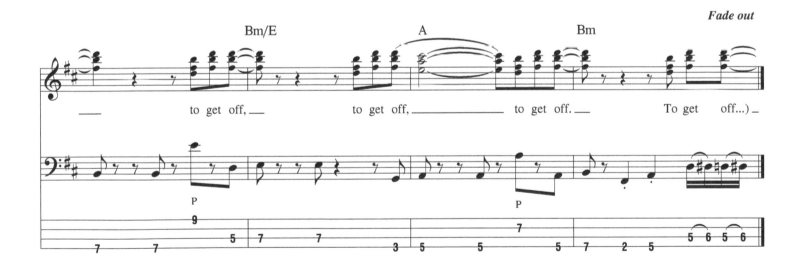

___ to get off, ___ to get off, ___ to get off. ___ To get off...) ___

Additional Lyrics

2. Lookin' through her dress, that drives me crazy
And makes me get off.
Sensuality excites my mind
And makes me get off.
If I were you, I'd get a good perspective
On how to get off.
Love me wild and love me crazy,
So we can get off.

Cissy Strut

By Arthur Neville, Leo Nocentelli, George Porter and Joseph Modeliste, Jr.

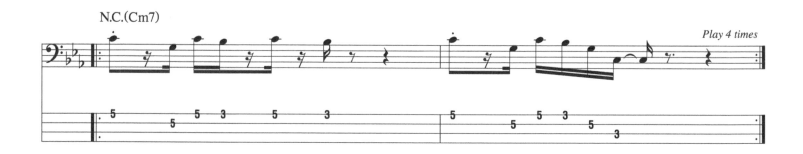

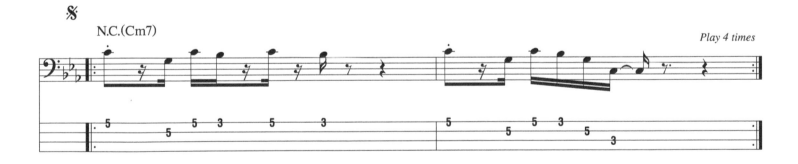

Get Up (I Feel Like Being) A Sex Machine

Words and Music by James Brown, Bobby Byrd and Ronald Lenhoff

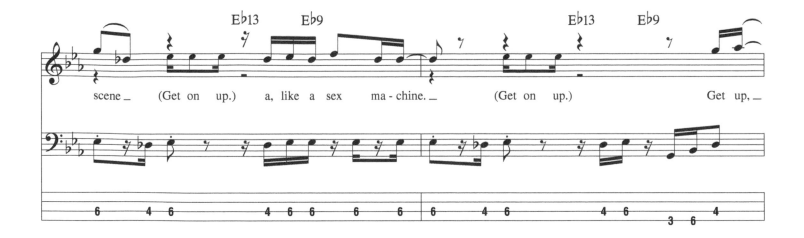

scene _ (Get on up.) a, like a sex ma - chine. _ (Get on up.) Get up, _

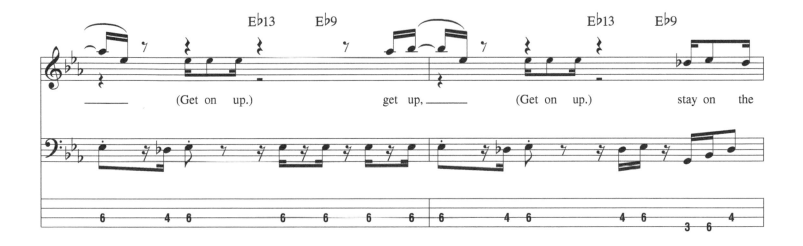

_____ (Get on up.) get up, _____ (Get on up.) stay on the

scene (Get on up.) a, like a sex ma - chine. _____ (Get on up.) Get up,

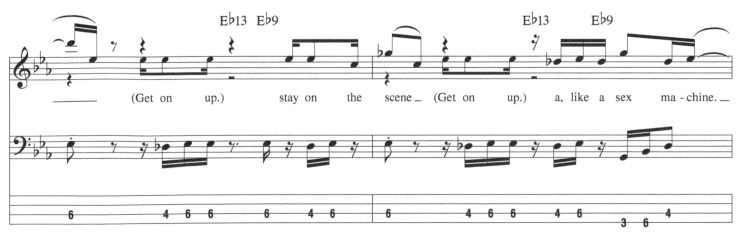

_____ (Get on up.) stay on the scene _ (Get on up.) a, like a sex ma - chine. _

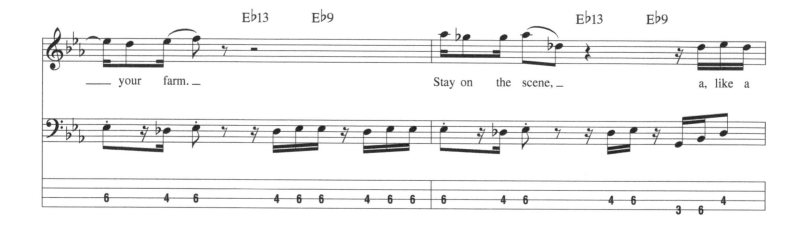

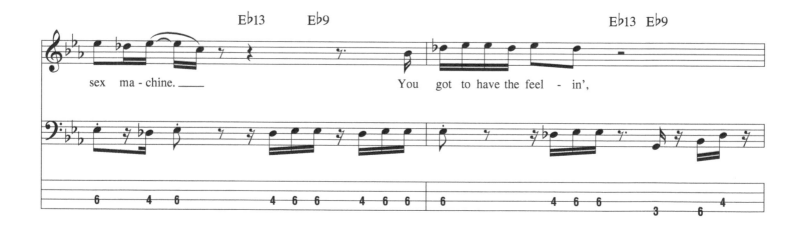

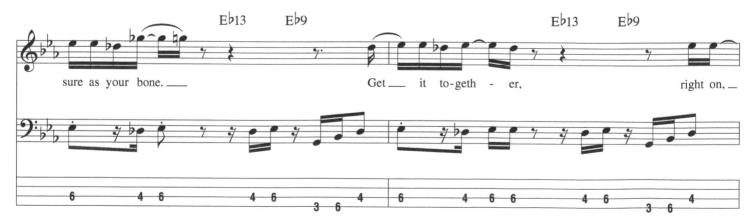

right on. Get up, (Get on up.) get up,

(Get on up.) get up. (Get on up.)

Interlude

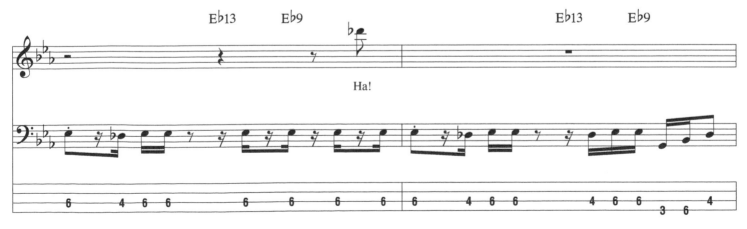

Ha!

Chorus

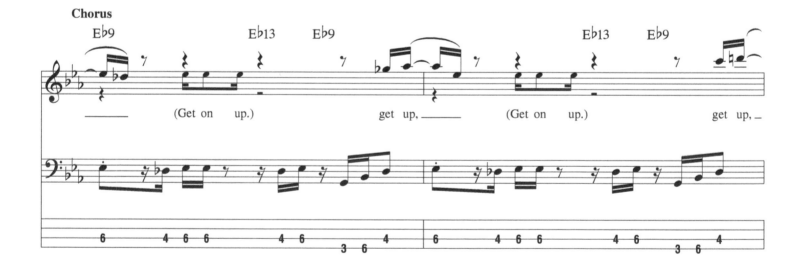

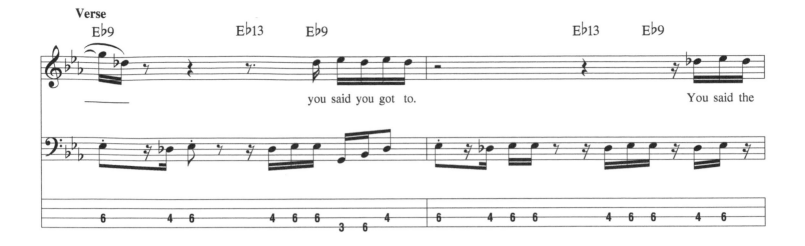

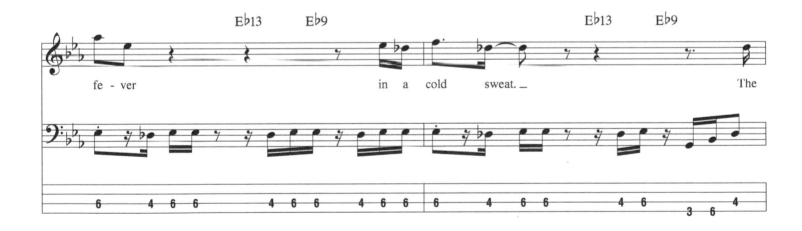

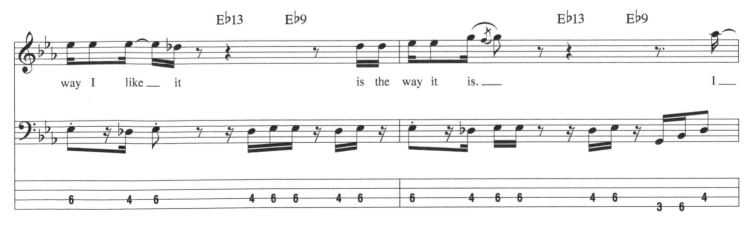

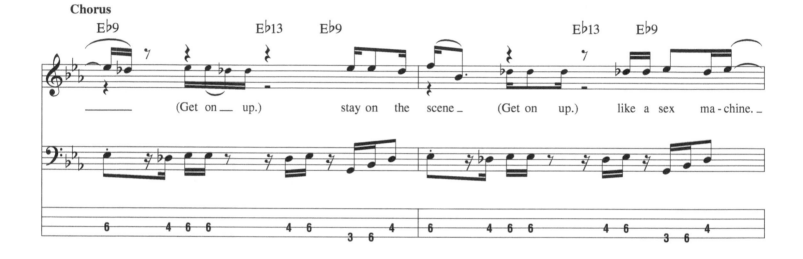

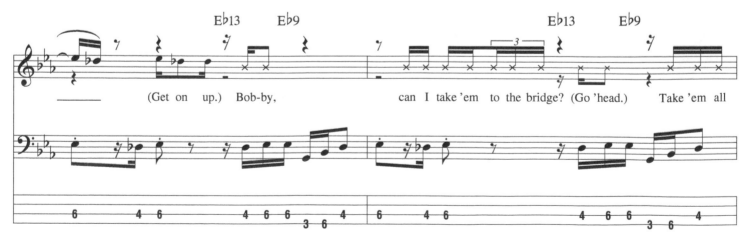

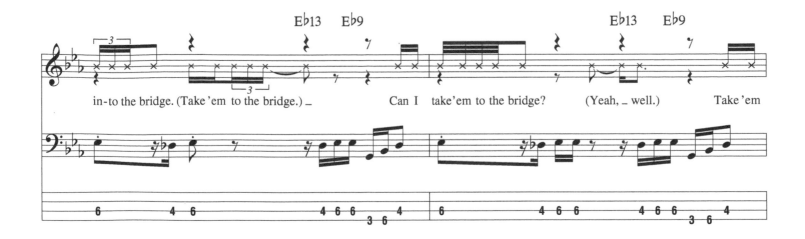

in-to the bridge. (Take 'em to the bridge.) ___   Can I take 'em to the bridge?   (Yeah, _ well.)   Take 'em

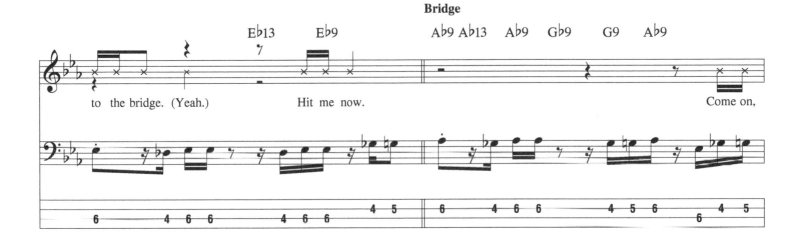

Bridge

to the bridge. (Yeah.)   Hit me now.   Come on,

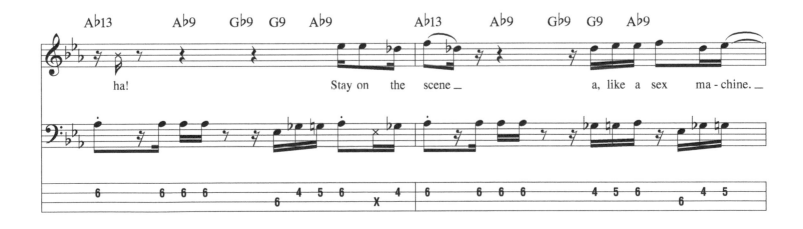

ha!   Stay on the scene ___   a, like a sex ma - chine. ___

___   The way I like ___ it   is the way it is. ___

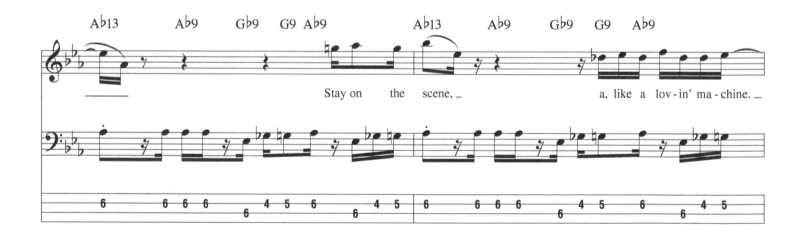

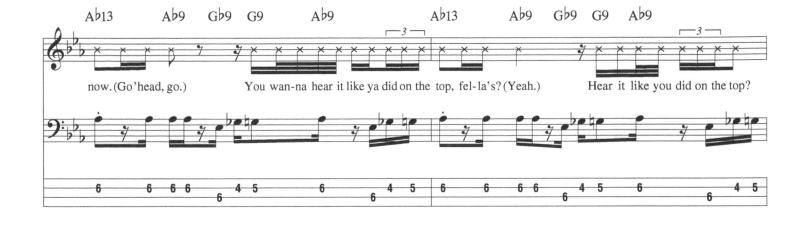

now. (Go' head, go.) You wan-na hear it like ya did on the top, fel-la's? (Yeah.) Hear it like you did on the top?

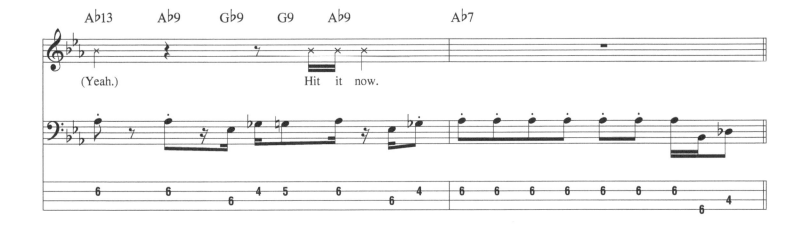

(Yeah.) Hit it now.

Chorus

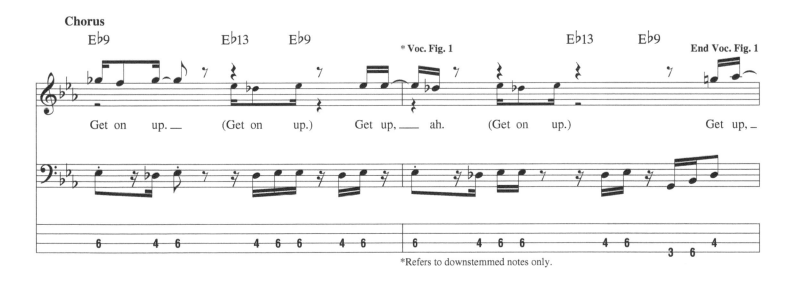

Get on up. __ (Get on up.) Get up, __ ah. (Get on up.) Get up, __

*Refers to downstemmed notes only.

Bkgd. Voc.: w/ Voc. Fig. 1 (9 times)

__ ah. Get on up, __ ah. Stay on the

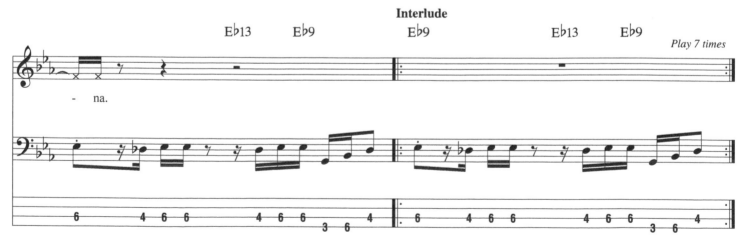

34

Chorus

Bkgd. Voc.: w/ Voc. Fig. 1 (6 times)

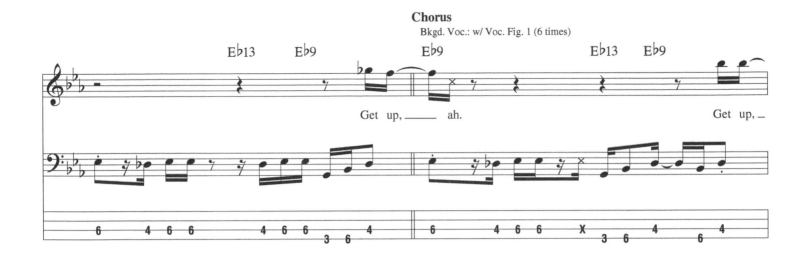

Get up, _____ ah.   Get up, _

_____ ah.   Stay on the scene   a, like a sex ma - chine, _

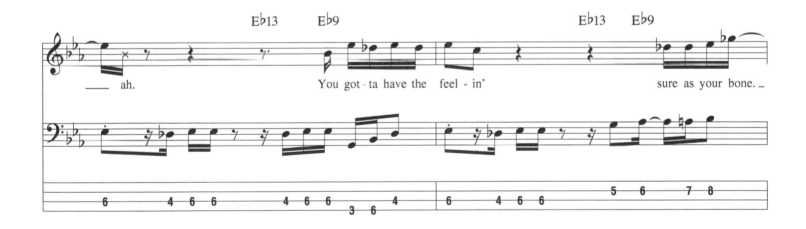

_____ ah.   You got - ta have the feel - in'   sure as your bone. _

_____   Get it _____ to - geth - er,   right on, _

Bkgd. Voc.: w/ Voc. Fig. 1 (2 times)

Interlude

Shake your mon - ey mak - er. Shake your mon - ey mak - er.

Shake your mon - ey mak - er. Shake your mon - ey mak - er.

Chorus

Bkgd. Voc.: w/ Voc. Fig. 1 (5 times)

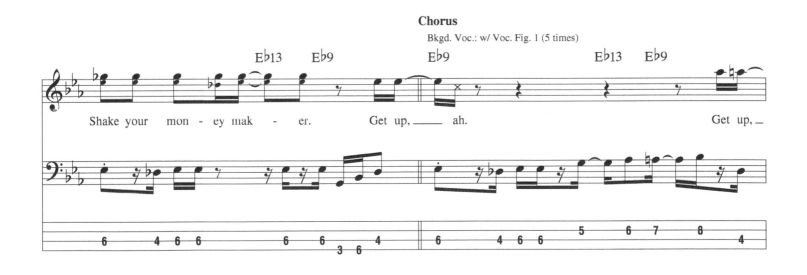

Shake your mon - ey mak - er. Get up, ___ ah. Get up, ___

___ ah. Get up, ___ ah. Get up! ___

Outro

Spoken: Can we hit it like we did one more time, from the top?

Can we hit it like that one more time?   One more time!   Let's hit it and quit!

(Go ahead!)   Can we hit it and quit?   Can we hit it and quit?   Can we hit it and

(Yeah!)   *(Yeah!)*

quit?   Hit it!

(Yeah!)

Higher Ground

Words and Music by Stevie Wonder

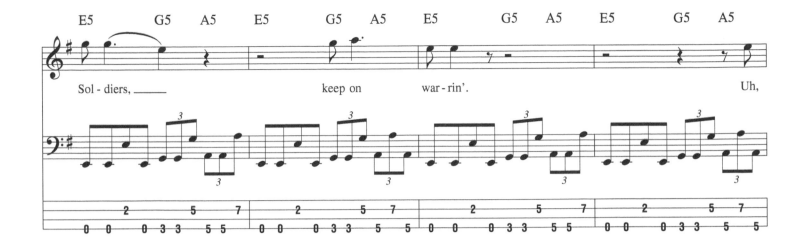

Sol - diers, _____ keep on war - rin'. Uh,

world, _____ keep on turn - in', ___

'cause it won't ___ be too long.

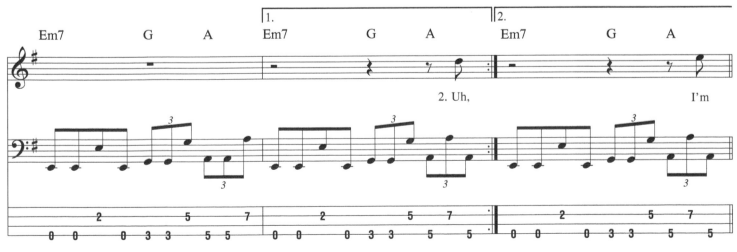

2. Uh, I'm

Chorus

so darn glad he let me try it a-gain, ___ 'cause my last time on earth I lived a

whole world of sin. ___ I'm so glad that I ___ know more than I knew then. ___ Gon-na

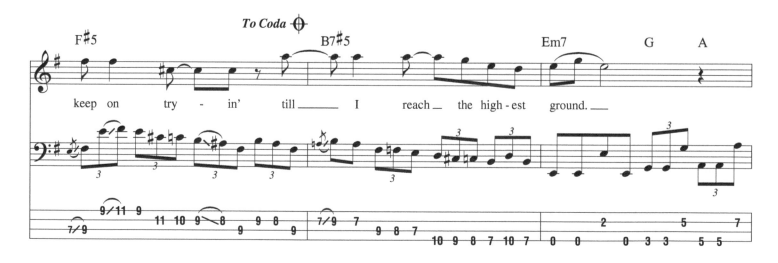

To Coda ⊕

keep on try-in' till ___ I reach ___ the high-est ground. ___

D.S. al Coda
(take repeat)

3. Uh,

steady gliss.

*Vocal disregards tempo change.

Additional Lyrics

2. Uh, powers a keep on lyin',
   While your people a keep on dyin'.
   Uh, world, keep on turnin',
   'Cause it won't be too long.

3. Uh, teachers, a keep on teachin'.
   Uh, preachers, a keep on preachin'.
   World, keep on turnin',
   'Cause it won't be too long. Oh, no!

4. Lovers, a keep on lovin',
   While believers keep on believin'.
   Sleepers, just stop sleepin',
   'Cause it won't be too long. Oh, no!

Le Freak

Words and Music by Nile Rodgers and Bernard Edwards

sure you'll be a-mazed. ___ Big fun ___ to be had by ev-'ry-one. ___

2nd & 3rd times, substitute Fill 1

It's up to you, ___ it sure-ly can be done. ___ Young and old are

do-in' it ___ I'm told. Just one try and you too will be sold. ___

Fill 1

It's called "Le Freak," they're do-in' it night and day. _____ Al - low us, we'll

To Coda

Chorus

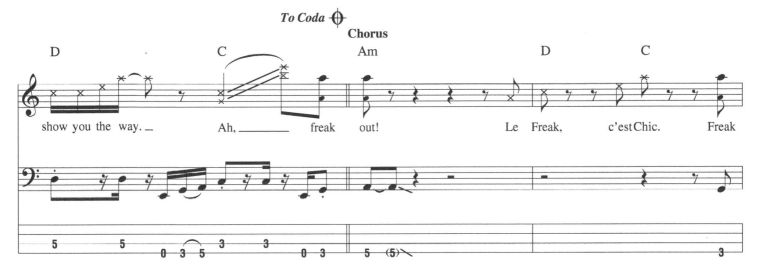

show you the way. _____ Ah, _____ freak out! Le Freak, c'est Chic. Freak

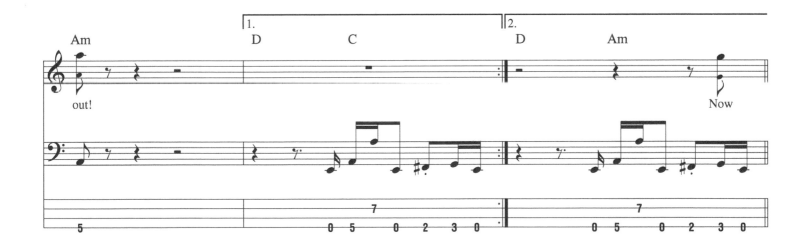

out! Now

Interlude

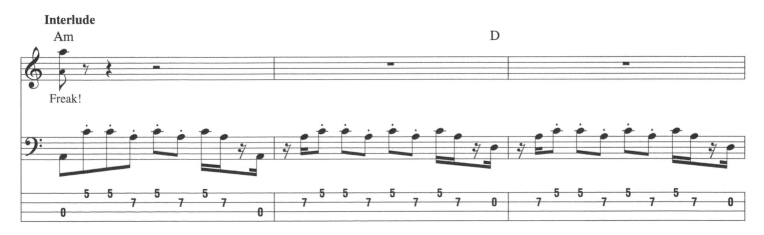

Freak!

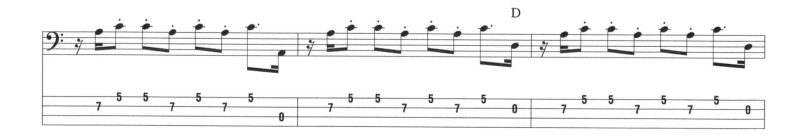

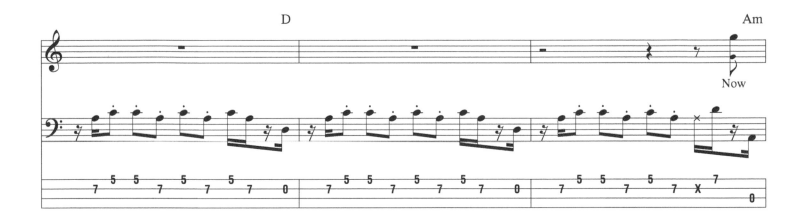

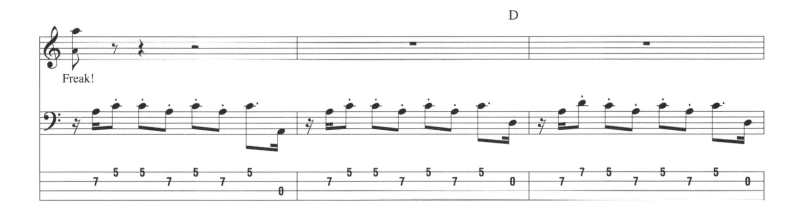

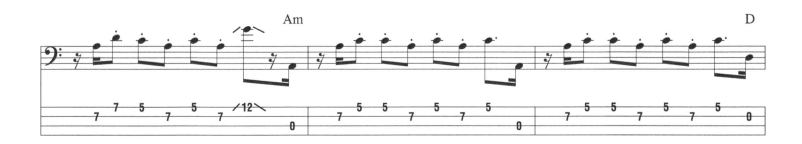

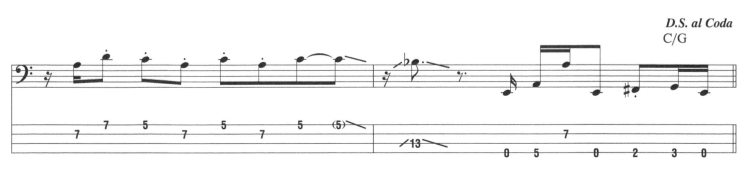

⊕ Coda

Outro-Chorus

out!   Le   Freak,   c'est Chic.   Freak   out!

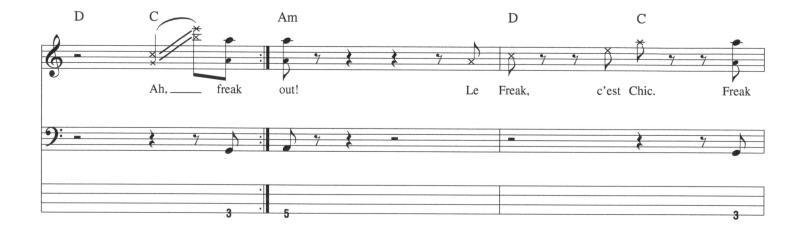

Ah, _____ freak   out!   Le   Freak,   c'est Chic.   Freak

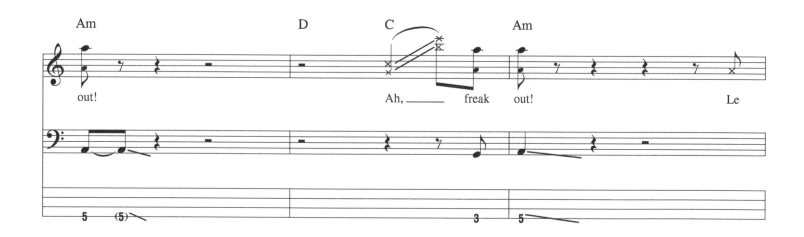

out!   Ah, _____ freak   out!   Le

Freak,   c'est Chic.   Freak   out!   Ah, _____ freak

out!   Le   Freak,   c'est Chic.   Freak   out!

Ah, _____ freak out!   Le   Freak,   c'est Chic.   Freak

Repeat and fade

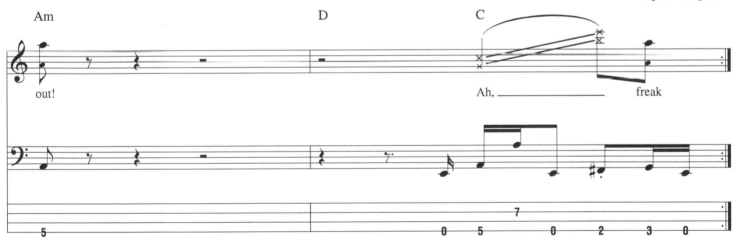

out!   Ah, _____ freak

Additional Lyrics

2., 3. All that pressure got you down,
      Has your head spinning all around.
      Feel the rhythm, chant the rhyme.
      Come on along and have a real good time.
      Like the days of stompin' at the Savoy,
      Now we Freak. Oh, what a joy.
      Just come on down to the 54,
      Find a spot out on the floor.

Pick Up the Pieces

Words and Music by James Hamish Stuart, Alan Gorrie, Roger Ball, Robbie McIntosh, Owen McIntyre and Malcolm Duncan

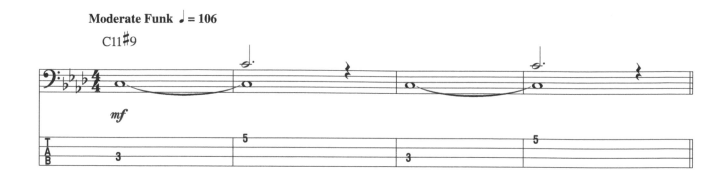

Fm7

D.S. al Coda

Coda

B♭11

C7#9

Fm7

Pick up   the piec - es.   Pick up the piec - es.

Pick up the piec - es.   Woo.   Pick up the

piec - es.   Ow! ___

Super Freak

Words and Music by Rick James and Alonzo Miller

girl. She likes the boys in the band. ___ She says that

I'm her all-time fa-v'rite. When I make my move to her room it's the

right time. She's nev-er hard ___ to please. ___ Oh, ___ no. That

𝄋 Pre-Chorus

girl is pret-ty { wild ___ now. } The kind of girl ___ you read ___ a-bout...
{ kink - y. }

(The girl's a su-per freak. ...in

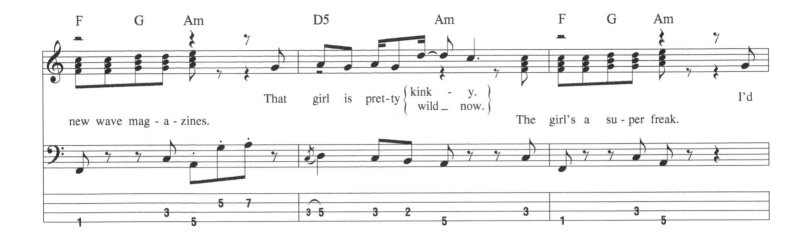

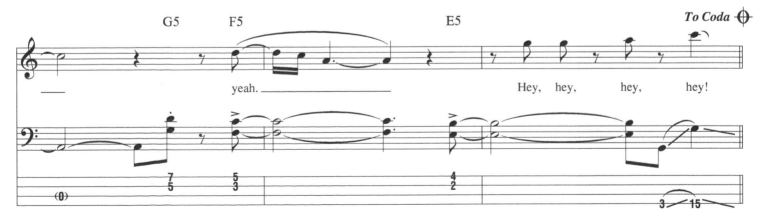

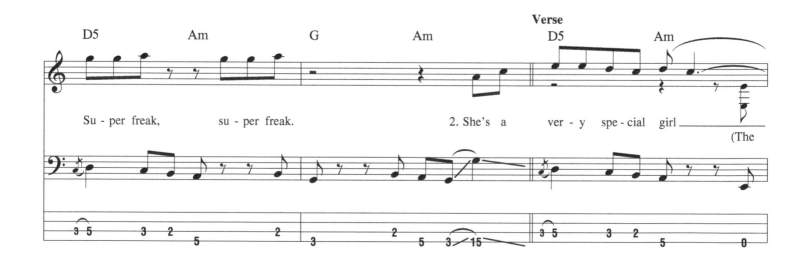

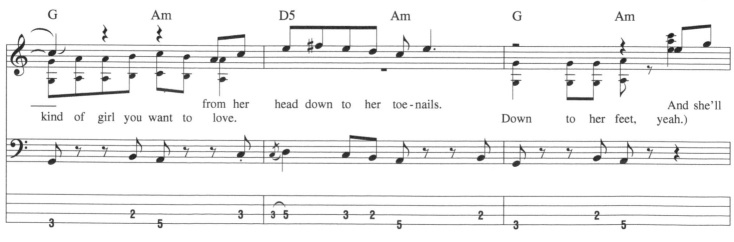

wait for me back-stage with her girl - friends in a lim-ou-sine. __

Three's not a crowd to her. __ She says, __ "Room sev - en -
(Long and black and shin-ing bright. Mé - nage à trois, we love you.

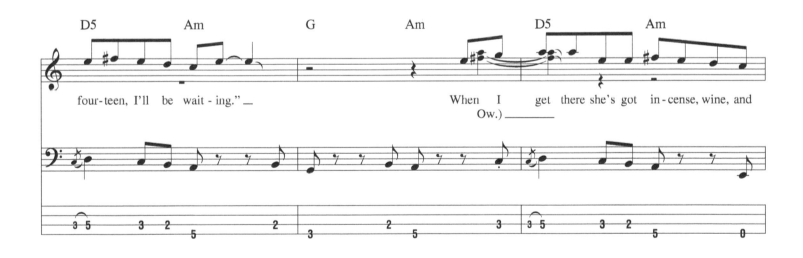

four-teen, I'll be wait - ing." __ When I get there she's got in - cense, wine, and
Ow.) _____

D.S. al Coda

can - dles. It's such a freak-y __ scene. __ That

Coda

Interlude

She's a su-per freak, su-per freak.

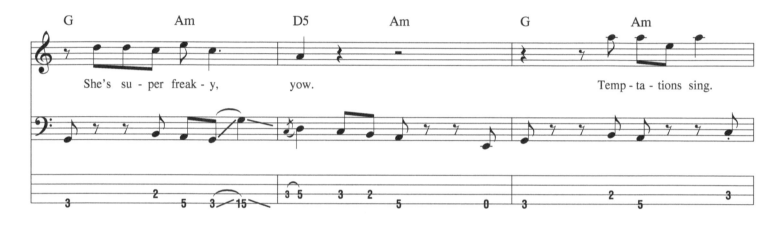

She's su-per freak-y, yow. Temp-ta-tions sing.

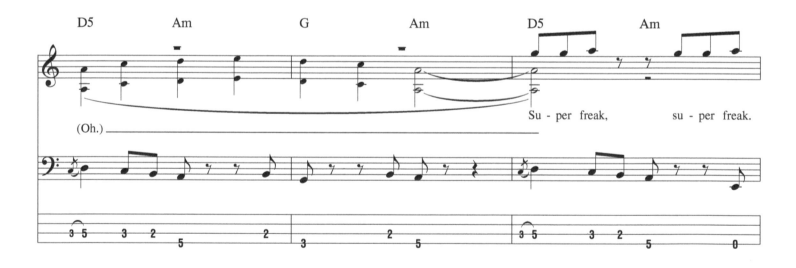

(Oh.) _____ Su-per freak, su-per freak.

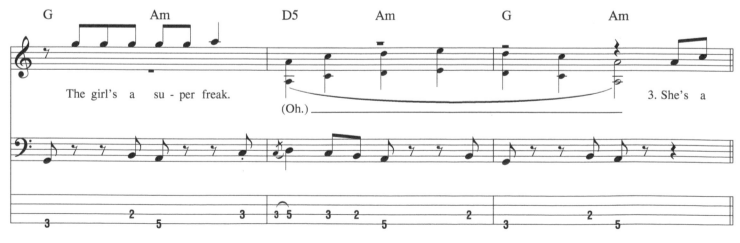

The girl's a su-per freak. (Oh.) _____ 3. She's a

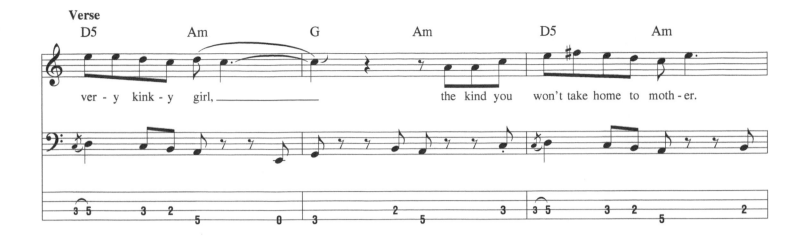

Verse

very kink-y girl, _____ the kind you won't take home to moth-er.

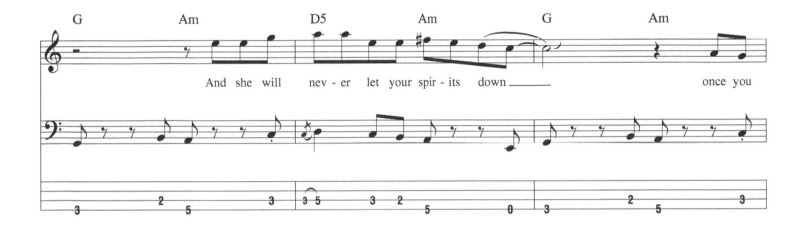

And she will nev-er let your spir-its down _____ once you

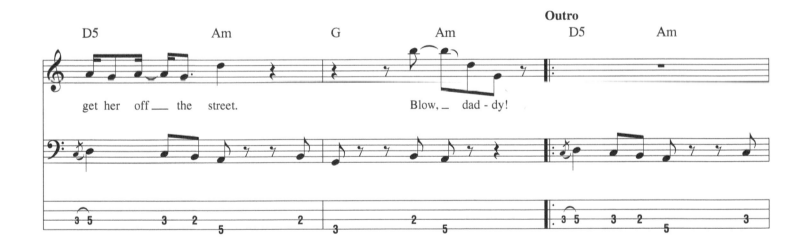

Outro

get her off _____ the street. Blow, _ dad-dy!

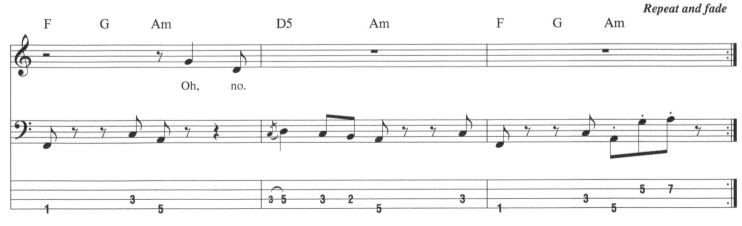

Repeat and fade

Oh, no.

HAL•LEONARD® BASS PLAY-ALONG

The Bass Play-Along™ Series will help you play your favorite songs quickly and easily! Just follow the tab, listen to the audio to hear how the bass should sound, and then play-along using the separate backing tracks. The melody and lyrics are also included in the book in case you want to sing, or to simply help you follow along. The audio files are enhanced so you can adjust the recording to any tempo without changing pitch!

1. Rock
00699674 Book/Online Audio $16.99
2. R&B
00699675 Book/Online Audio $16.99
3. Songs for Beginners
00346426 Book/Online Audio $16.99
4. '90s Rock
00294992 Book/Online Audio $16.99
5. Funk
00699680 Book/Online Audio $16.99
6. Classic Rock
00699678 Book/Online Audio $17.99
8. Punk Rock
00699813 Book/CD Pack $12.95
9. Blues
00699817 Book/Online Audio $16.99
10. Jimi Hendrix – Smash Hits
00699815 Book/Online Audio $17.99
11. Country
00699818 Book/CD Pack $12.95
12. Punk Classics
00699814 Book/CD Pack $12.99
13. The Beatles
00275504 Book/Online Audio $17.99
14. Modern Rock
00699821 Book/CD Pack $14.99
15. Mainstream Rock
00699822 Book/CD Pack $14.99
16. '80s Metal
00699825 Book/CD Pack $16.99
17. Pop Metal
00699826 Book/CD Pack $14.99
18. Blues Rock
00699828 Book/CD Pack $19.99
19. Steely Dan
00700203 Book/Online Audio $17.99
20. The Police
00700270 Book/Online Audio $19.99
21. Metallica: 1983-1988
00234338 Book/Online Audio $19.99
22. Metallica: 1991-2016
00234339 Book/Online Audio $19.99

23. Pink Floyd –
Dark Side of The Moon
00700847 Book/Online Audio $16.99
24. Weezer
00700960 Book/CD Pack $17.99
25. Nirvana
00701047 Book/Online Audio $17.99
26. Black Sabbath
00701180 Book/Online Audio $17.99
27. Kiss
00701181 Book/Online Audio $17.99
28. The Who
00701182 Book/Online Audio $19.99
29. Eric Clapton
00701183 Book/Online Audio $17.99
30. Early Rock
00701184 Book/CD Pack $15.99
31. The 1970s
00701185 Book/CD Pack $14.99
32. Cover Band Hits
00211598 Book/Online Audio $16.99
33. Christmas Hits
00701197 Book/CD Pack $12.99
34. Easy Songs
00701480 Book/Online Audio $17.99
35. Bob Marley
00701702 Book/Online Audio $17.99
36. Aerosmith
00701886 Book/CD Pack $14.99
37. Modern Worship
00701920 Book/Online Audio $19.99
38. Avenged Sevenfold
00702386 Book/CD Pack $16.99
39. Queen
00702387 Book/Online Audio $17.99

40. AC/DC
14041594 Book/Online Audio $17.99
41. U2
00702582 Book/Online Audio $19.99
42. Red Hot Chili Peppers
00702991 Book/Online Audio $19.99
43. Paul McCartney
00703079 Book/Online Audio $19.99
44. Megadeth
00703080 Book/CD Pack $16.99
45. Slipknot
00703201 Book/CD Pack $17.99
46. Best Bass Lines Ever
00103359 Book/Online Audio $19.99
47. Dream Theater
00111940 Book/Online Audio $24.99
48. James Brown
00117421 Book/CD Pack $16.99
49. Eagles
00119936 Book/Online Audio $17.99
50. Jaco Pastorius
00128407 Book/Online Audio $17.99
51. Stevie Ray Vaughan
00146154 Book/CD Pack $16.99
52. Cream
00146159 Book/Online Audio $19.99
56. Bob Seger
00275503 Book/Online Audio $16.99
57. Iron Maiden
00278398 Book/Online Audio $17.99
58. Southern Rock
00278436 Book/Online Audio $17.99

HAL•LEONARD®

Prices, contents, and availability subject to change without notice.

Visit Hal Leonard Online at **www.halleonard.com**